Hey, Good Lookin!

Whatcha Got Cookin'?

Meal Planning Organizer

Copyright 2016

Meal Planner

	Breakfast	Lunch	Dinner
Monday			
Tuesday			
Wednesday			
Thursaday			
Friday			
Saturday			
Sunday			

things to buy :   things to do :

Meal Planner

	Breakfast	Lunch	Dinner
Monday			
Tuesday			
Wednesday			
Thursaday			
Friday			
Saturday			
Sunday			

things to buy :   things to do :

Meal Planner

	Breakfast	Lunch	Dinner
Monday			
Tuesday			
Wednesday			
Thursaday			
Friday			
Saturday			
Sunday			

things to buy :   things to do :

Meal Planner

	Breakfast	Lunch	Dinner
Monday			
Tuesday			
Wednesday			
Thursaday			
Friday			
Saturday			
Sunday			

things to buy :   things to do :

Meal Planner

	Breakfast	Lunch	Dinner
Monday			
Tuesday			
Wednesday			
Thursaday			
Friday			
Saturday			
Sunday			

things to buy :

things to do :

Meal Planner

	Breakfast	Lunch	Dinner
Monday			
Tuesday			
Wednesday			
Thursaday			
Friday			
Saturday			
Sunday			

things to buy :   things to do :

Meal Planner

	Breakfast	Lunch	Dinner
Monday			
Tuesday			
Wednesday			
Thursaday			
Friday			
Saturday			
Sunday			

things to buy :   things to do :

Meal Planner

	Breakfast	Lunch	Dinner
Monday			
Tuesday			
Wednesday			
Thursaday			
Friday			
Saturday			
Sunday			

things to buy :   things to do :

Meal Planner

	Breakfast	Lunch	Dinner
Monday			
Tuesday			
Wednesday			
Thursaday			
Friday			
Saturday			
Sunday			

things to buy :   things to do :

Meal Planner

	Breakfast	Lunch	Dinner
Monday			
Tuesday			
Wednesday			
Thursaday			
Friday			
Saturday			
Sunday			

things to buy :

things to do :

Meal Planner

	Breakfast	Lunch	Dinner
Monday			
Tuesday			
Wednesday			
Thursaday			
Friday			
Saturday			
Sunday			

things to buy :   things to do :

Meal Planner

	Breakfast	Lunch	Dinner
Monday			
Tuesday			
Wednesday			
Thursaday			
Friday			
Saturday			
Sunday			

things to buy :

things to do :

Meal Planner

	Breakfast	Lunch	Dinner
Monday			
Tuesday			
Wednesday			
Thursaday			
Friday			
Saturday			
Sunday			

things to buy :   things to do :

Meal Planner

	Breakfast	Lunch	Dinner
Monday			
Tuesday			
Wednesday			
Thursaday			
Friday			
Saturday			
Sunday			

things to buy :   things to do :

Meal Planner

	Breakfast	Lunch	Dinner
Monday			
Tuesday			
Wednesday			
Thursaday			
Friday			
Saturday			
Sunday			

things to buy :   things to do :

Meal Planner

	Breakfast	Lunch	Dinner
Monday			
Tuesday			
Wednesday			
Thursaday			
Friday			
Saturday			
Sunday			

things to buy :   things to do :

Meal Planner

	Breakfast	Lunch	Dinner
Monday			
Tuesday			
Wednesday			
Thursaday			
Friday			
Saturday			
Sunday			

things to buy :   things to do :

Meal Planner

	Breakfast	Lunch	Dinner
Monday			
Tuesday			
Wednesday			
Thursaday			
Friday			
Saturday			
Sunday			

things to buy :   things to do :

Meal Planner

	Breakfast	Lunch	Dinner
Monday			
Tuesday			
Wednesday			
Thursaday			
Friday			
Saturday			
Sunday			

things to buy :   things to do :

Meal Planner

	Breakfast	Lunch	Dinner
Monday			
Tuesday			
Wednesday			
Thursaday			
Friday			
Saturday			
Sunday			

things to buy :   things to do :

Meal Planner

	Breakfast	Lunch	Dinner
Monday			
Tuesday			
Wednesday			
Thursaday			
Friday			
Saturday			
Sunday			

things to buy :   things to do :

Meal Planner

	Breakfast	Lunch	Dinner
Monday			
Tuesday			
Wednesday			
Thursaday			
Friday			
Saturday			
Sunday			

things to buy :　　　　　things to do :

Meal Planner

	Breakfast	Lunch	Dinner
Monday			
Tuesday			
Wednesday			
Thursaday			
Friday			
Saturday			
Sunday			

things to buy :   things to do :

Meal Planner

	Breakfast	Lunch	Dinner
Monday			
Tuesday			
Wednesday			
Thursaday			
Friday			
Saturday			
Sunday			

things to buy :   things to do :

Meal Planner

	Breakfast	Lunch	Dinner
Monday			
Tuesday			
Wednesday			
Thursaday			
Friday			
Saturday			
Sunday			

things to buy : things to do :

Meal Planner

	Breakfast	Lunch	Dinner
Monday			
Tuesday			
Wednesday			
Thursaday			
Friday			
Saturday			
Sunday			

things to buy :   things to do :

Meal Planner

	Breakfast	Lunch	Dinner
Monday			
Tuesday			
Wednesday			
Thursaday			
Friday			
Saturday			
Sunday			

things to buy :   things to do :

Meal Planner

	Breakfast	Lunch	Dinner
Monday			
Tuesday			
Wednesday			
Thursaday			
Friday			
Saturday			
Sunday			

things to buy :   things to do :

Meal Planner

	Breakfast	Lunch	Dinner
Monday			
Tuesday			
Wednesday			
Thursaday			
Friday			
Saturday			
Sunday			

things to buy :   things to do :

Meal Planner

	Breakfast	Lunch	Dinner
Monday			
Tuesday			
Wednesday			
Thursaday			
Friday			
Saturday			
Sunday			

things to buy :   things to do :

Meal Planner

	Breakfast	Lunch	Dinner
Monday			
Tuesday			
Wednesday			
Thursaday			
Friday			
Saturday			
Sunday			

things to buy :   things to do :

Meal Planner

	Breakfast	Lunch	Dinner
Monday			
Tuesday			
Wednesday			
Thursaday			
Friday			
Saturday			
Sunday			

things to buy :

things to do :

Meal Planner

	Breakfast	Lunch	Dinner
Monday			
Tuesday			
Wednesday			
Thursaday			
Friday			
Saturday			
Sunday			

things to buy :

things to do :

Meal Planner

	Breakfast	Lunch	Dinner
Monday			
Tuesday			
Wednesday			
Thursaday			
Friday			
Saturday			
Sunday			

things to buy :   things to do :

Meal Planner

	Breakfast	Lunch	Dinner
Monday			
Tuesday			
Wednesday			
Thursaday			
Friday			
Saturday			
Sunday			

things to buy :   things to do :

Meal Planner

	Breakfast	Lunch	Dinner
Monday			
Tuesday			
Wednesday			
Thursaday			
Friday			
Saturday			
Sunday			

things to buy :   things to do :

Meal Planner

	Breakfast	Lunch	Dinner
Monday			
Tuesday			
Wednesday			
Thursaday			
Friday			
Saturday			
Sunday			

things to buy :　　　　　　　things to do :

Meal Planner

	Breakfast	Lunch	Dinner
Monday			
Tuesday			
Wednesday			
Thursaday			
Friday			
Saturday			
Sunday			

things to buy : things to do :

Meal Planner

	Breakfast	Lunch	Dinner
Monday			
Tuesday			
Wednesday			
Thursaday			
Friday			
Saturday			
Sunday			

things to buy :   things to do :

Meal Planner

	Breakfast	Lunch	Dinner
Monday			
Tuesday			
Wednesday			
Thursaday			
Friday			
Saturday			
Sunday			

things to buy :

things to do :

Meal Planner

	Breakfast	Lunch	Dinner
Monday			
Tuesday			
Wednesday			
Thursaday			
Friday			
Saturday			
Sunday			

things to buy :   things to do :

Meal Planner

	Breakfast	Lunch	Dinner
Monday			
Tuesday			
Wednesday			
Thursaday			
Friday			
Saturday			
Sunday			

things to buy :   things to do :

Meal Planner

	Breakfast	Lunch	Dinner
Monday			
Tuesday			
Wednesday			
Thursaday			
Friday			
Saturday			
Sunday			

things to buy :   things to do :

Meal Planner

	Breakfast	Lunch	Dinner
Monday			
Tuesday			
Wednesday			
Thursaday			
Friday			
Saturday			
Sunday			

things to buy :   things to do :

Meal Planner

	Breakfast	Lunch	Dinner
Monday			
Tuesday			
Wednesday			
Thursaday			
Friday			
Saturday			
Sunday			

things to buy :

things to do :

Meal Planner

	Breakfast	Lunch	Dinner
Monday			
Tuesday			
Wednesday			
Thursaday			
Friday			
Saturday			
Sunday			

things to buy : things to do :

Meal Planner

	Breakfast	Lunch	Dinner
Monday			
Tuesday			
Wednesday			
Thursaday			
Friday			
Saturday			
Sunday			

things to buy :　　　　　things to do :

Meal Planner

	Breakfast	Lunch	Dinner
Monday			
Tuesday			
Wednesday			
Thursaday			
Friday			
Saturday			
Sunday			

things to buy :

things to do :

Meal Planner

	Breakfast	Lunch	Dinner
Monday			
Tuesday			
Wednesday			
Thursaday			
Friday			
Saturday			
Sunday			

things to buy :
things to do :

Meal Planner

	Breakfast	Lunch	Dinner
Monday			
Tuesday			
Wednesday			
Thursaday			
Friday			
Saturday			
Sunday			

things to buy :   things to do :

Meal Planner

	Breakfast	Lunch	Dinner
Monday			
Tuesday			
Wednesday			
Thursaday			
Friday			
Saturday			
Sunday			

things to buy :   things to do :

Meal Planner

	Breakfast	Lunch	Dinner
Monday			
Tuesday			
Wednesday			
Thursaday			
Friday			
Saturday			
Sunday			

things to buy :   things to do :

Meal Planner

	Breakfast	Lunch	Dinner
Monday			
Tuesday			
Wednesday			
Thursaday			
Friday			
Saturday			
Sunday			

things to buy :   things to do :

Meal Planner

	Breakfast	Lunch	Dinner
Monday			
Tuesday			
Wednesday			
Thursaday			
Friday			
Saturday			
Sunday			

things to buy :   things to do :

Meal Planner

	Breakfast	Lunch	Dinner
Monday			
Tuesday			
Wednesday			
Thursaday			
Friday			
Saturday			
Sunday			

things to buy :   things to do :

Meal Planner

	Breakfast	Lunch	Dinner
Monday			
Tuesday			
Wednesday			
Thursaday			
Friday			
Saturday			
Sunday			

things to buy :   things to do :

Meal Planner

	Breakfast	Lunch	Dinner
Monday			
Tuesday			
Wednesday			
Thursaday			
Friday			
Saturday			
Sunday			

things to buy :   things to do :

Meal Planner

	Breakfast	Lunch	Dinner
Monday			
Tuesday			
Wednesday			
Thursaday			
Friday			
Saturday			
Sunday			

things to buy :

things to do :

Meal Planner

	Breakfast	Lunch	Dinner
Monday			
Tuesday			
Wednesday			
Thursaday			
Friday			
Saturday			
Sunday			

things to buy :   things to do :

Meal Planner

	Breakfast	Lunch	Dinner
Monday			
Tuesday			
Wednesday			
Thursaday			
Friday			
Saturday			
Sunday			

things to buy :　　　　things to do :

Meal Planner

	Breakfast	Lunch	Dinner
Monday			
Tuesday			
Wednesday			
Thursaday			
Friday			
Saturday			
Sunday			

things to buy :   things to do :

Meal Planner

	Breakfast	Lunch	Dinner
Monday			
Tuesday			
Wednesday			
Thursaday			
Friday			
Saturday			
Sunday			

things to buy :   things to do :

Meal Planner

	Breakfast	Lunch	Dinner
Monday			
Tuesday			
Wednesday			
Thursaday			
Friday			
Saturday			
Sunday			

things to buy :   things to do :

Meal Planner

	Breakfast	Lunch	Dinner
Monday			
Tuesday			
Wednesday			
Thursaday			
Friday			
Saturday			
Sunday			

things to buy :   things to do :

Meal Planner

	Breakfast	Lunch	Dinner
Monday			
Tuesday			
Wednesday			
Thursaday			
Friday			
Saturday			
Sunday			

things to buy :   things to do :

Meal Planner

	Breakfast	Lunch	Dinner
Monday			
Tuesday			
Wednesday			
Thursaday			
Friday			
Saturday			
Sunday			

things to buy :　　　　　things to do :

Meal Planner

	Breakfast	Lunch	Dinner
Monday			
Tuesday			
Wednesday			
Thursaday			
Friday			
Saturday			
Sunday			

things to buy :   things to do :

Meal Planner

	Breakfast	Lunch	Dinner
Monday			
Tuesday			
Wednesday			
Thursaday			
Friday			
Saturday			
Sunday			

things to buy :   things to do :

Meal Planner

	Breakfast	Lunch	Dinner
Monday			
Tuesday			
Wednesday			
Thursaday			
Friday			
Saturday			
Sunday			

things to buy :　　　　　things to do :

Meal Planner

	Breakfast	Lunch	Dinner
Monday			
Tuesday			
Wednesday			
Thursaday			
Friday			
Saturday			
Sunday			

things to buy :   things to do :

Meal Planner

	Breakfast	Lunch	Dinner
Monday			
Tuesday			
Wednesday			
Thursaday			
Friday			
Saturday			
Sunday			

things to buy :   things to do :

Meal Planner

	Breakfast	Lunch	Dinner
Monday			
Tuesday			
Wednesday			
Thursaday			
Friday			
Saturday			
Sunday			

things to buy :   things to do :

Meal Planner

	Breakfast	Lunch	Dinner
Monday			
Tuesday			
Wednesday			
Thursaday			
Friday			
Saturday			
Sunday			

things to buy :   things to do :

Meal Planner

	Breakfast	Lunch	Dinner
Monday			
Tuesday			
Wednesday			
Thursaday			
Friday			
Saturday			
Sunday			

things to buy :   things to do :

Meal Planner

	Breakfast	Lunch	Dinner
Monday			
Tuesday			
Wednesday			
Thursaday			
Friday			
Saturday			
Sunday			

things to buy :   things to do :

Meal Planner

	Breakfast	Lunch	Dinner
Monday			
Tuesday			
Wednesday			
Thursaday			
Friday			
Saturday			
Sunday			

things to buy :   things to do :

Meal Planner

	Breakfast	Lunch	Dinner
Monday			
Tuesday			
Wednesday			
Thursaday			
Friday			
Saturday			
Sunday			

things to buy :   things to do :

Meal Planner

	Breakfast	Lunch	Dinner
Monday			
Tuesday			
Wednesday			
Thursaday			
Friday			
Saturday			
Sunday			

things to buy :

things to do :

Meal Planner

	Breakfast	Lunch	Dinner
Monday			
Tuesday			
Wednesday			
Thursaday			
Friday			
Saturday			
Sunday			

things to buy :

things to do :

Meal Planner

	Breakfast	Lunch	Dinner
Monday			
Tuesday			
Wednesday			
Thursaday			
Friday			
Saturday			
Sunday			

things to buy :   things to do :

Meal Planner

	Breakfast	Lunch	Dinner
Monday			
Tuesday			
Wednesday			
Thursaday			
Friday			
Saturday			
Sunday			

things to buy :   things to do :

Meal Planner

	Breakfast	Lunch	Dinner
Monday			
Tuesday			
Wednesday			
Thursaday			
Friday			
Saturday			
Sunday			

things to buy :

things to do :

Meal Planner

	Breakfast	Lunch	Dinner
Monday			
Tuesday			
Wednesday			
Thursaday			
Friday			
Saturday			
Sunday			

things to buy :   things to do :

Meal Planner

	Breakfast	Lunch	Dinner
Monday			
Tuesday			
Wednesday			
Thursaday			
Friday			
Saturday			
Sunday			

things to buy :   things to do :

Meal Planner

	Breakfast	Lunch	Dinner
Monday			
Tuesday			
Wednesday			
Thursaday			
Friday			
Saturday			
Sunday			

things to buy :

things to do :

Meal Planner

	Breakfast	Lunch	Dinner
Monday			
Tuesday			
Wednesday			
Thursaday			
Friday			
Saturday			
Sunday			

things to buy :　　　　　things to do :

Meal Planner

	Breakfast	Lunch	Dinner
Monday			
Tuesday			
Wednesday			
Thursaday			
Friday			
Saturday			
Sunday			

things to buy :　　　　　things to do :

Meal Planner

	Breakfast	Lunch	Dinner
Monday			
Tuesday			
Wednesday			
Thursaday			
Friday			
Saturday			
Sunday			

things to buy :   things to do :

Meal Planner

	Breakfast	Lunch	Dinner
Monday			
Tuesday			
Wednesday			
Thursaday			
Friday			
Saturday			
Sunday			

things to buy :   things to do :

Meal Planner

	Breakfast	Lunch	Dinner
Monday			
Tuesday			
Wednesday			
Thursaday			
Friday			
Saturday			
Sunday			

things to buy :

things to do :

Meal Planner

	Breakfast	Lunch	Dinner
Monday			
Tuesday			
Wednesday			
Thursaday			
Friday			
Saturday			
Sunday			

things to buy :   things to do :

Meal Planner

	Breakfast	Lunch	Dinner
Monday			
Tuesday			
Wednesday			
Thursaday			
Friday			
Saturday			
Sunday			

things to buy :   things to do :

Meal Planner

	Breakfast	Lunch	Dinner
Monday			
Tuesday			
Wednesday			
Thursaday			
Friday			
Saturday			
Sunday			

things to buy :   things to do :

Meal Planner

	Breakfast	Lunch	Dinner
Monday			
Tuesday			
Wednesday			
Thursaday			
Friday			
Saturday			
Sunday			

things to buy :   things to do :

Meal Planner

	Breakfast	Lunch	Dinner
Monday			
Tuesday			
Wednesday			
Thursaday			
Friday			
Saturday			
Sunday			

things to buy :   things to do :

Meal Planner

	Breakfast	Lunch	Dinner
Monday			
Tuesday			
Wednesday			
Thursaday			
Friday			
Saturday			
Sunday			

things to buy :   things to do :

Meal Planner

	Breakfast	Lunch	Dinner
Monday			
Tuesday			
Wednesday			
Thursaday			
Friday			
Saturday			
Sunday			

things to buy :   things to do :

Meal Planner

	Breakfast	Lunch	Dinner
Monday			
Tuesday			
Wednesday			
Thursaday			
Friday			
Saturday			
Sunday			

things to buy :   things to do :

Meal Planner

	Breakfast	Lunch	Dinner
Monday			
Tuesday			
Wednesday			
Thursaday			
Friday			
Saturday			
Sunday			

things to buy :   things to do :

Meal Planner

	Breakfast	Lunch	Dinner
Monday			
Tuesday			
Wednesday			
Thursaday			
Friday			
Saturday			
Sunday			

things to buy :   things to do :

Meal Planner

	Breakfast	Lunch	Dinner
Monday			
Tuesday			
Wednesday			
Thursaday			
Friday			
Saturday			
Sunday			

things to buy :   things to do :

Meal Planner

	Breakfast	Lunch	Dinner
Monday			
Tuesday			
Wednesday			
Thursaday			
Friday			
Saturday			
Sunday			

things to buy :   things to do :

Meal Planner

	Breakfast	Lunch	Dinner
Monday			
Tuesday			
Wednesday			
Thursaday			
Friday			
Saturday			
Sunday			

things to buy :   things to do :

Meal Planner

	Breakfast	Lunch	Dinner
Monday			
Tuesday			
Wednesday			
Thursaday			
Friday			
Saturday			
Sunday			

things to buy :

things to do :